D1359937

Bridgestone
B O O K S

World of Insects

Grasshoppers

by Connie Colwell Miller

Consultant:
Gary A. Dunn, MS, Director of Education
Young Entomologists' Society Inc.
Lansing, Michigan

Capstone
press

Mankato, Minnesota

Bridgestone Books are published by Capstone Press,
151 Good Counsel Drive, P.O. Box 669, Mankato, Minnesota 56002.
www.capstonepress.com

Library of Congress Cataloging-in-Publication Data
Miller, Connie Colwell, 1976–
    Grasshoppers / by Connie Colwell Miller.
        p. cm.—(Bridgestone books. World of insects)
    Includes bibliographical references and index.
    ISBN 0-7368-3708-6 (hardcover)
    1. Grasshoppers—Juvenile literature. I. Title. II. Series.
QL508.A2M54 2005
595.7'26—dc22   2004013428

Summary: A brief introduction to grasshoppers, discussing their characteristics, habitat, life cycle, and
    predators. Includes a range map, life cycle illustration, and amazing facts.

Editorial Credits
Erika L. Shores, editor; Jennifer Bergstrom, set designer; Erin Scott, Wylde Hare Creative, illustrator;
    Jo Miller, photo researcher; Scott Thoms, photo editor

Photo Credits
Brand X Pictures, back cover
Bruce Coleman Inc., 18; Jane Burton, 16
Corel, 1
Digital Vision, cover
Dwight R. Kuhn, 20
Index Stock Imagery /Zefa Visual Media, 4
Pete Carmichael, 6
Rob Curtis, 10, 12

1 2 3 4 5 6 10 09 08 07 06 05

Table of Contents

4

Grasshoppers

Grasshoppers can jump the length of a hopscotch court in one leap. They can jump as high as a basketball hoop. Grasshoppers have springlike knees and strong muscles in their back legs.

Grasshoppers are insects. Katydids and crickets are related to grasshoppers. Katydids, crickets, and grasshoppers have wings and six legs. Males make sounds using their legs and wings.

◄ Grasshoppers use their strong back legs to leap through the air.

What Grasshoppers Look Like

Adult grasshoppers can be 1 to 5 inches (3 to 13 centimeters) long. A hard outer covering called an **exoskeleton** protects a grasshopper's soft body.

Grasshopper bodies have three sections called the head, **thorax**, and **abdomen**. Two **antennas** are on the head. The thorax is the middle section. Four wings and six legs are joined to the thorax. The abdomen is the end part of the body. Grasshoppers breathe air through holes along their thorax and abdomen.

◄ Some grasshoppers are the color of their surroundings. Grasshoppers are yellow, red, black, brown, or green.

Grasshopper Range Map

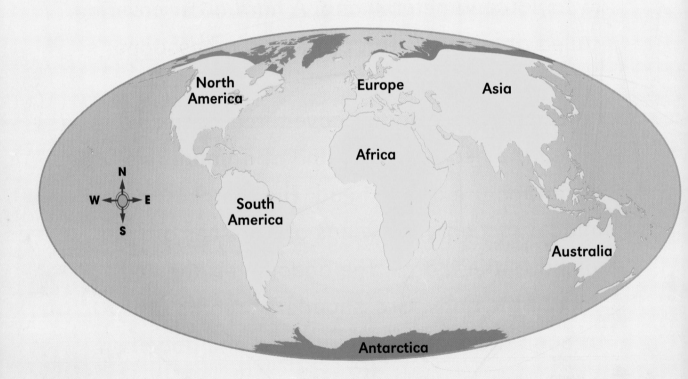

North America

Europe

Asia

Africa

South America

Australia

Antarctica

N
W   E
S

☐ Where Grasshoppers Live

Grasshoppers in the World

About 23,000 kinds of grasshoppers live around the world. North America is home to 1,000 different kinds of grasshoppers. Places like Antarctica and the Arctic are too cold for grasshoppers.

◄ Grasshoppers live in many places around the world.

Grasshopper Habitats

Grasshoppers live wherever plants grow. Grasshopper **habitats** include fields, meadows, and forests. Grasshoppers can survive cool and dry weather if they have enough plants to eat.

Grasshoppers are active during the day. They hop around to look for food. They stay warm in the sun. At night, grasshoppers rest on plants.

◀ Grasshoppers live in grassy areas.

What Grasshoppers Eat

Grasshoppers eat plants. They like softer leaves like lettuce better than tree leaves. Grasshoppers do not eat animals or insects.

Grasshoppers can cause trouble for farmers. Grasshoppers eat farm crops like corn and alfalfa. Hungry grasshoppers sometimes travel together to find food. These large groups are called **swarms**. Grasshopper swarms can quickly destroy entire fields of crops.

◄ Grasshoppers have strong jaws that chew from side to side.

Life Cycle of a Grasshopper

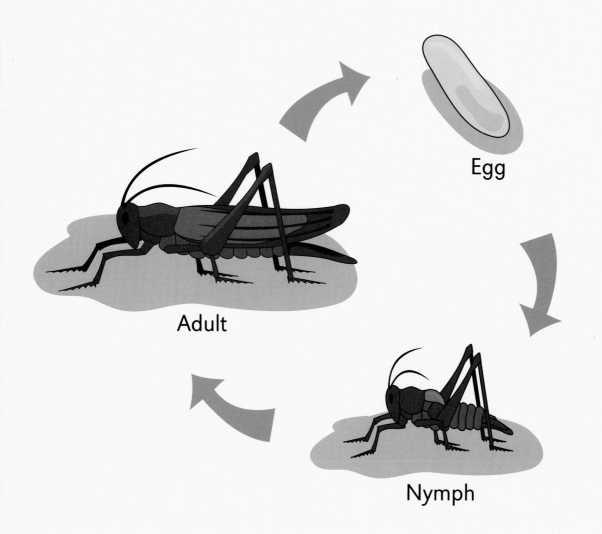

Egg

Adult

Nymph

Eggs and Nymphs

In summer or fall, female and male grasshoppers mate. Females then dig a hole in the ground. They lay from two to 100 eggs in the hole. They then squirt a sticky liquid on top of the eggs. The liquid plugs the hole and protects the eggs.

Grasshopper **nymphs** hatch from eggs in the spring. Nymphs look and act like small grasshoppers. But nymphs don't have full-grown wings until they are adults.

Molting into an Adult

Nymphs begin to grow after they hatch. The nymphs shed, or **molt**, their exoskeletons when their outer coverings become too small.

Nymphs begin to grow wings. The wings start as tiny buds. Nymphs cannot fly until their wings are fully grown. They must run or jump to avoid danger.

Grasshopper nymphs molt five or more times before becoming adults. Most nymphs become adults 40 to 60 days after hatching.

◄ Grasshopper nymphs, like the one at right, look like small adults.

Dangers to Grasshoppers

Grasshoppers have many **predators**. Lizards, birds, and spiders eat grasshoppers. People also eat grasshoppers. In some parts of the world, grasshoppers are a tasty treat.

Eggs and nymphs also face dangers. Some flies lay their eggs on grasshopper eggs. When the flies hatch, they eat the eggs. Beetles, birds, lizards, and rodents often eat nymphs.

Grasshoppers may face some dangers. But they continue to live around the world.

◀ Lizards grab grasshoppers with their long tongues.

Amazing Facts about Grasshoppers

- Grasshoppers sometimes spit brown juice to scare away predators.
- A grasshopper has many six-sided lenses in its two large eyes. With these compound eyes, the insect can see to the front, back, and side.
- Grasshoppers do not have ears. They have organs on their legs that hear sounds.
- A grasshopper uses all six legs when it walks. The front legs also hold food while it eats.

◄ Some people call the brown juice a grasshopper spits "tobacco juice."

Glossary

abdomen (AB-duh-muhn)—the end section of an insect's body

antenna (an-TEN-uh)—a feeler on an insect's head

exoskeleton (eks-oh-SKEL-uh-tuhn)—the hard covering on the outside of an insect

habitat (HAB-uh-tat)—the place and natural conditions in which plants and animals live

molt (MOHLT)—to shed an outer layer of skin, or exoskeleton, so a new exoskeleton can be seen

nymph (NIMF)—a young form of an insect; nymphs change into adults by molting several times.

predator (PRED-uh-tur)—an animal that hunts other animals for food

swarm (SWORM)—a group of insects that gather and move in large numbers

thorax (THOR-aks)—the middle section of an insect's body

Read More

Heinrichs, Ann. *Grasshoppers*. Nature's Friends. Minneapolis: Compass Point Books. Minneapolis, 2002.

Miller, Sara Swan. *Grasshoppers and Crickets of North America.* Animals in Order. New York: Franklin Watts, 2002.

Internet Sites

FactHound offers a safe, fun way to find Internet sites related to this book. All of the sites on FactHound have been researched by our staff.

Here's how:
1. Visit *www.facthound.com*
2. Type in this special code **0736837086** for age-appropriate sites. Or enter a search word related to this book for a more general search.
3. Click on the **Fetch It** button.

FactHound will fetch the best sites for you!

Index